The Liberty Bell

By Lloyd G. Douglas

Welcome Books™

SCHOLASTIC INC.

New York Toronto London Auckland Sydney
Mexico City New Delhi Hong Kong Buenos Aires

Photo Credits: Cover © Leif Skoogfors/Corbis; p. 5 © Lester Lefkowitz/Corbis;
pp. 7, 17 © Bettmann/Corbis; p. 9 © National Archive and Records Administration; p. 11 © Bequest
of Mrs. Benjamin Ogle/Corbis; p. 13 © Ed Eckstein/Corbis; p. 15 © Hulton Archive/Getty Images;
p. 19 © H. Armstrong Roberts; p. 21 © Bob Krist/Corbis
Contributing Editor: Jennifer Silate
Book Design: Christopher Logan

ISBN 0-516-24485-X

12 11 10 9 8 7 6   4 5 6 7 8/0

Printed in the U.S.A.   61

First Scholastic paperback printing, September 2003

Contents

The **Liberty** Bell is an American **symbol**.

It is a symbol of **freedom** in America.

PROCLAIM LIB
USE IN PHILADA BY ORDER OF
PASS AND STOW
PHILADA
MDCCLIII

5

The Liberty Bell was made in 1752.

It was made to **celebrate** the **constitution** of Pennsylvania.

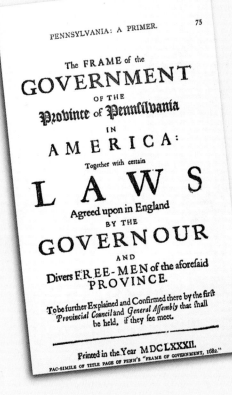

The FRAME of the

GOVERNMENT

OF THE

Province of Pennsilvania

IN

AMERICA:

Together with certain

LAWS

Agreed upon in England

BY THE

GOVERNOUR

AND

Divers FREE-MEN of the aforesaid
PROVINCE.

To be further Explained and Confirmed there by the first
Provincial Council and *General Assembly* that shall
be held, if they see meet.

Printed in the Year MDCLXXXII.

FAC-SIMILE OF TITLE PAGE OF PENN'S "FRAME OF GOVERNMENT," 1682."

The Liberty Bell was **rung** many times.

In 1776, it was rung to celebrate the **Declaration of Independence**.

9

The last time the Liberty Bell rang was in 1846.

It was rung for George Washington's birthday.

The Liberty Bell has a big **crack** in it.

It does not ring anymore.

13

The Liberty Bell has been taken around the country.

Many people have seen it.

15

An American space ship was named after the Liberty Bell.

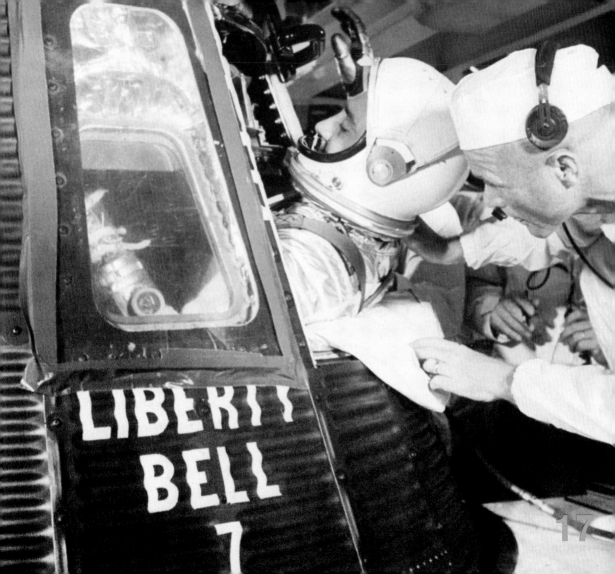

LIBERTY BELL 7

A picture of the Liberty Bell is on a **coin**.

Many people visit the Liberty Bell each year.

It is an important American symbol.

THE NEOF LEV XXV VIII [...]
[...] HOUSE IN PHILAD [...]

PASS AND [...]
PHILAD [...]
[...]

21

New Words

celebrate (**sel**-uh-brate) to do something fun on a special occasion

coin (**koin**) a piece of metal with a picture and a number on it that is used as money

constitution (kon-stuh-**too**-shuhn) the system of laws in a country or state that tells the rights of the people and the powers of the government

crack (**krak**) a very thin break in something

Declaration of Independence (dek-luh-**ray**-shuhn **uhv** in-di-**pen**-duhnss) a document declaring the freedom of the thirteen American colonies from British rule

freedom (**free**-duhm) being able to go where you want or do what you want

liberty (**lib**-ur-tee) freedom

rung (**ruhng**) having made a clear musical sound

symbol (**sim**-buhl) a drawing or an object that stands for something else

To Find Out More

Web Site
A to Z Kid's Stuff: Symbols of the USA
http://www.atozkidsstuff.com/symbols.html
Read facts and print a picture of the Liberty Bell and other American symbols to color on this Web site.

Index

About the Author
Lloyd G. Douglas is an editor and writer of children's books.

Reading Consultants
Kris Flynn, Coordinator, Small School District Literacy, The San Diego County
   Office of Education

Shelly Forys, Certified Reading Recovery Specialist, W.J. Zahnow Elementary
   School, Waterloo, IL

Sue McAdams, Former President of the North Texas Reading Council of the
   IRA, and Early Literacy Consultant, Dallas, TX